The Forgotten Song of the Romantic Poets

Edited by
David C. Jones

THE FORGOTTEN SONG OF THE ROMANTIC POETS

EDITED BY

DAVID C. JONES

DEDICATION

To poets, truth-seekers

MERCI

To my son, Wesley T. Jones for designing and formatting this book, for creating the cover and the map, and for his wisdom.

The Forgotten Song of the Romantic Poets

Calgary, AB, Canada

ISBN 978-1-7388171-0-8

Published by David C. Jones

Cover by Wesley T. Jones

For the cover portrait of Victor Hugo, I thank the artist, Auguste Rodin (1840-1917), the gift of Edmond C. Bonaventure, and the Cooper Hewitt Smithsonian Design Museum.

CONTENTS

INTRODUCTION—FORGOTTEN SONG

Sadly, the world forgets itself, forgets especially its moments of melody and uplift. With each passing generation, the memory of these moments recedes. My purpose here is to rescue the forgotten song of the Romantic poets. I sang it when I was young, and I sing I now more passionately when I am old—the radiance of the fields, the company of virtues, the beams of love, the glow of beauty, the stirring of wisdom—all the lyrics here, in single refrains and epigrams, in poetry and prose. For a world swirling with dissension and division, the song needs remembering.

Listen to the poets who expressed its light and urgency. Why poets? The French Romantic, Alphonse de Lamartine, answered: "Poetry has been the guardian angel of humanity in all ages." "Poetry lifts the veil from the hidden beauty of the world," said Percy Bysshe Shelley. "Poetry thus makes immortal all that is best and most beautiful in the world."

Happiness, joy, and peace go together with good poetry, Samuel Taylor Coleridge knew: "When a man is unhappy, he writes damned bad poetry, I find. Poetry has been to me its own, exceeding great reward; it has given me the habit of wishing to discover the good and beautiful in all that meets and surrounds me." He added, "No man was ever yet a great poet, without being at the same time a profound philosopher."

William Blake went deeper—"Every man who is not an artist is a traitor to his own nature....God is the poetic genius in each of us."

VERSE 1 —

OVERTURE

WILLIAM BLAKE

"In the universe, there are things that are known,
and things that are unknown, and in between
there are doors."

ROBERT BROWNING

"Truth is within ourselves; it takes no rise
From outward things, whate'er you may believe
There is an inmost centre in us all,
Where truth abides in fullness."

VICTOR HUGO

"I am a soul. I know well that what I shall render
up to the grave is not myself. That which is myself
will go elsewhere. Earth, thou art not my abyss!"

ROBERT BROWNING

"To do good things in the world, first you must know who you are and what gives meaning to your life."

VICTOR HUGO

"Well, for us, in history where goodness is a rare pearl, he who was good almost takes precedence over he who was great."

JOHN KEATS

"Nothing ever becomes real till experienced—even a proverb is no proverb until your life has illustrated it."

"For axioms in philosophy are not axioms until they are proved upon our pulses."

"Life is but a day: a fragile dewdrop on its perilous way from a tree's summit."

ROBERT BROWNING

"As is your sort of mind, so is your sort of search. You will find what you desire."

WILLIAM BLAKE

"As we are, so we see."

PERCY BYSSHE SHELLEY

"The mind is its own place, and of itself can make a heaven of hell, a hell of heaven."

ELIZABETH BARRETT BROWNING

"Why, what is to live? Not to eat and drink and breathe—but to feel the life in you down all the fibres of being, passionately and joyfully."

VICTOR HUGO

"Man's greatest actions are performed in minor struggles. Life, misfortune, isolation, abandonment and poverty are battlefields which have their heroes—obscure heroes who are at times greater than illustrious heroes."

SAMUEL TAYLOR COLERIDGE

"The happiness of life is made up of minute fractions—the little, soon-forgotten charities of a kiss, a smile, a kind look, a heartfelt compliment in the disguise of a playful raillery, and the countless other infinitesimals of pleasant thought and feeling."

VICTOR HUGO

"The little people must be sacred to the big ones, and it is from the rights of the weak that the duty of the strong is comprised."

SAMUEL TAYLOR COLERIDGE

"The first great requisite is absolute sincerity. Falsehood and disguise are miseries and misery-makers."

ANNA LAETITIA BARBAULT

"This dead of midnight is the noon of thought,
And Wisdom mounts her zenith with the stars.
At this still hour the self-collected soul
Turns inward, and beholds a stranger there
Of high descent, and more than mortal rank;
An embryo God; a spark of fire divine."

ELIZABETH BARRETT BROWNING

"God's gifts put men's best dreams to shame."

ANNA LAETITIA BARBAULT

"While Genius was thus wasting his strength in eccentric flights, I saw a person of a very different appearance, named Application."

VERSE 2—

VIRTUES

VICTOR HUGO

"Virtue has a veil, vice a mask."

"Kindness is virtue itself."

ROBERT BROWNING

"It's wiser being good than bad;
It's safer being meek than fierce;
It's fitter being sane than mad.
My own hope is, a sun will pierce
The thickest cloud earth ever stretched...."

ALPHONSE DE LAMARTINE

"Void of freedom, what would virtue be?"

VICTOR HUGO

ACTION

"As with stomachs, we should pity minds that do not eat."

"Not being heard is no reason for silence."

"There comes an hour when protest no longer suffices; after philosophy there must be action; the strong hand finishes what the idea has sketched."

WILLIAM WORDSWORTH

BLESSINGS

"A deep distress hath humanised my soul."

WILLIAM WORDSWORTH

BLISS

"Bliss it was in that dawn to be alive
But to be young was very heaven."

WILLIAM WORDSWORTH

CHEERFULNESS

"A cheerful life is what the Muses love,
A soaring spirit is their prime delight."

VICTOR HUGO

"Is it not a thing divine to have a smile which, none know how, has the power to lighten the weight of that enormous chain which all the living in common drag behind them?"

"Cheerfulness is like money well expended in charity; the more we dispense of it, the greater our possession."

ELIZABETH BARRETT BROWNING CLARITY

"Yes, I answered you last night;
No, this morning, sir, I say:
Colour seen by candle-light
Will not look the same by day."

VICTOR HUGO COMPLIMENTING

"A compliment is something like a kiss through a veil."

LORD BYRON CONSISTENCY

"I have no consistency, except in politics; and that probably arises from my indifference to the subject altogether."

VICTOR HUGO

CONSCIENCE

"You ask me what forces me to speak?
A strange thing: my conscience."

ANNA LETITIA BARBAULD

CONVICTIONS

"The most characteristic mark of a great mind is to choose some one important object and pursue it for life."

PERCY BYSSHE SHELLEY

DELIGHT

"I love all that thou lovest,
Spirit of Delight!
The fresh Earth in new leaves dressed,
And the starry night;
Autumn evening, and the morn
When the golden mists are born."

SAMUEL TAYLOR COLERIDGE

"I have often thought what a melancholy world this would be without children, and what an inhuman world without the aged."

VICTOR HUGO

"The delight we inspire in others has this enchanting peculiarity that, far from being diminished like every other reflection, it returns to us more radiant than ever."

ANNA LAETITIA BARBAULD

"Let us confess a truth, humiliating to human pride—a very small part only of the opinions of the coolest philosopher are the result of fair reasoning; the rest are formed by his education, his temperament, by the age in which he lives, by trains of thought directed to a particular track through some accidental association—in short by prejudice."

ELIZABETH BARRETT BROWNING

"Better far
Pursue a frivolous trade by serious means
Than a sublime art frivolously."

ANNA LAETITIA BARBAULD

"If an author would have us feel a strong degree of compassion, his characters must not be too perfect."

LORD BYRON

"Men think highly of those who rise rapidly in the world; whereas nothing rises quicker than dust, straw, and feathers."

ALPHONSE DE LAMARTINE

ELOQUENCE

"Eloquence dwells quite as much in the hearts as on the lips of the orator."

WILLIAM WORDSWORTH

EMPATHY

"Thanks to the human heart by which we live,
Thanks to its tenderness, its joys, and its fears,
To me the meanest flower that blows can give
Thoughts that do often lie too deep for tears."

WILLIAM BLAKE

"Can I see another's woe,
And not be in sorrow too?
Can I see another's grief
And not seek for kind relief?"

ALPHONSE DE LAMARTINE

ENTHUSIASM

"Enthusiasm is the intoxication of earnestness."

VICTOR HUGO

"Go out in the world and work like money doesn't matter, sing as if no one is listening, love as if you have never been hurt, and dance as if no one is watching."

WILLIAM WORDSWORTH

"Faith is a passionate intuition."

VICTOR HUGO

"A faith is a necessity to a man. Woe to him who believes in nothing."

"Be as a bird perched on a frail branch
that she feels bending beneath her,
still she sings away all the same,
knowing she has wings."

ANNA LETITIA BARBAULD

"But every act in consequence of our faith, strengthens faith."

ELIZABETH BARRETT BROWNING

"Earth's crammed with heaven, And
every common bush afire with God."

WILLIAM BLAKE

FAITHFULNESS

"Without unceasing practice nothing can be done. Practice is Art. If you leave off you are lost."

WILLIAM BLAKE

FORGIVENESS

"They who forgive most shall be most forgiven."

"The glory of Christianity is to conquer by forgiveness."

VICTOR HUGO

"If I were Jesus Christ, I would save Judas."

VICTOR HUGO

FRATERNITY

"Great perils have this beauty, that they bring to light the fraternity of strangers."

ALPHONSE DE LAMARTINE

"Sometimes only one person is missing, and the whole world seems depopulated."

VICTOR HUGO

FREEDOM TO DREAM

"If you don't build castles in the air, you won't build anything on the ground."

ROBERT BROWNING

FRIENDSHIP

"What a thing friendship is—World without end."

SAMUEL TAYLOR COLERIDGE

"Friendship is a sheltering tree."

LORD BYRON

"The poor dog, in life the firmest friend. The first to welcome, foremost to defend."

ANNA LAETITIA BARBAULD

"With regard to the choice of friends, there is little to say; for a friend is never chosen. A secret sympathy, the attraction of a thousand nameless qualities, a charm in the expression of the countenance, even in the voice or manner, a similarity of circumstances—these are the things that begin attachment."

CHARLES LAMB

'Tis the privilege of friendship to talk nonsense, and to have nonsense respected."

VICTOR HUGO

"Friendship exists outside our modern economy of scarcity.... It's not about apportioning vanishing resources of time and energy. Friendship is a blessed relic of the ancient economy of the gift, and the time freely given to people dear to you actually creates magical abundance."

CHARLES LAMB

"The going away of friends does not make the remainder more precious. It takes so much from them as there was a common link. A.B. and C. make a party. A. dies. B. not only loses A. but all A's part in C. C. loses A's part in B., and so the alphabet sickens by subtraction."

ANNA LAETITIA BARBAULD

"Happy is he to whom, in the mature season of life, there remains one tried and constant friend...."

WILLIAM WORDSWORTH

"Be mild and cleave to gentle things,
thy glory and thy happiness be there."

SAMUEL TAYLOR COLERIDGE

"Advice is like snow; the softer it falls,
the longer it dwells upon, and the
deeper it sinks into the mind."

ALPHONSE DE LAMARTINE

"A woman's strength is most potent
when robed in gentleness."

ROBERT BROWNING GIVING

"The best things in life can never be kept;
They must be given away.
A Smile, a Kiss, and Love."

VICTOR HUGO GRACE

"When grace is joined with wrinkles, it is adorable. There is an unspeakable dawn in happy, old age."

VICTOR HUGO

GRATITUDE

"The most beautiful of altars... is the soul of an unhappy creature consoled and thanking God."

"To give thanks in solitude is enough. Thanksgiving has wings and goes where it must go. Your prayer knows much more about it than you do."

WILLIAM BLAKE

"Gratitude is heaven itself; there could be no heaven without gratitude."

ROBERT BROWNING

GROWTH

"My business is not to remake myself, but to make the absolute best of what God made."

"Why stay on earth except to grow?"

CHARLES LAMB

"The greatest pleasure I know, is to do a good action by stealth, and to have it found out by accident."

SAMUEL TAYLOR COLERIDGE

"Nothing can permanently please, which doesn't contain in itself the reason why it is so, and not otherwise."

CHARLES LAMB

"You do not play then at whist, sir? Alas, what a sad old age you are preparing for yourself!"

LORD BYRON

"All who joy would win must share it.
Happiness was born a twin."

ALPHONSE DE LAMARTINE

"Joy is a flame which association alone can keep alive, and which goes out unless communicated."

WILLIAM BLAKE

"The busy bee has no time for sorrow."

VICTOR HUGO

"Happiness wishes everybody happy."

"Life's greatest happiness is to be convinced we are loved."

SAMUEL TAYLOR COLERIDGE

"We ne'er can be made happy by compulsion."

SAMUEL TAYLOR COLERIDGE HOLINESS

"A mother is a mother still,
The holiest thing alive."

VICTOR HUGO

"Word which the finger of God has written on the brow of every man—hope!"

"In joined hands there is still some token of hope, in the clenched fist none."

"There is no distress so complete but that even in the most critical moments the inexplicable sunrise of hope is seen in its depths."

CHARLOTTE TURNER SMITH

"For what is life, when Hope has ceas'd to strew
Her fragile flowers along its thorny way?"

ELIZABETH BARRETT BROWNING

"With stammering lips and insufficient sound I strive and struggle to deliver right the music of my nature."

SAMUEL TAYLOR COLERIDGE

"He is the best physician who is the most ingenious inspirer of hope."

SAMUEL TAYLOR COLERIDGE

"There is small chance of truth at the goal, where there is not childlike humility at the starting-post."

ELIZABETH BARRETT BROWNING

"The wisest word man reaches is the humblest he can speak."

ROBERT BROWNING

"As if true pride
Were not also humble!"

CHARLES LAMB

"A laugh is worth a hundred groans in any market."

SAMUEL TAYLOR COLERIDGE

"No mind is thoroughly well-organized that is deficient in a sense of humor."

"People of humor are always in some degree people of genius."

"The most happy marriage I can picture or imagine to myself would be the union of a deaf man to a blind woman."

CHARLES LAMB

"I always arrive late at the office, but I make up for it by leaving early."

ROBERT BROWNING

"There are three ways of learning golf: by study which is the most wearisome; by imitation, which is the most fallacious; and by experience, which is the most bitter."

"The trouble most of us find with the modern matched sets of clubs is that they don't really seem to know any more about the game than the old ones did."

WILLIAM BLAKE

"Those who restrain desire do so because theirs is weak enough to be restrained."

LORD BYRON

"I should, many a good day, have blown my brains out, but for the recollection that it would have given pleasure to my mother-in-law."

SAMUEL TAYLOR COLERIDGE

"Swans sing before they die— 't were no bad thing
Should certain persons die before they sing."

CHARLES LAMB

"A sweet child is the sweetest thing in nature.... Lawyers, I suppose, were children once."

"Here cometh April again, and as far as I can see the world hath more fools than ever."

VICTOR HUGO

INTEGRITY

"Morality is truth in full bloom."

ROBERT BROWNING

JUDGEMENT

"I judge people by what they might be—not are, nor will be."

VICTOR HUGO

JUSTICE

"Being good is easy, what is difficult is being just."

VICTOR HUGO

LIGHT

"If you look in the eyes of the young, you see flame. If you look in the eyes of the old, you see light."

VICTOR HUGO

MERCY

"Amnesty is as good for those who give it as for those who receive it. It has the admirable quality of bestowing mercy on both sides."

WILLIAM BLAKE

"Mercy is the golden chain by which society is bound together."

ALPHONSE DE LAMARTINE

MODESTY

"Modesty and dew love the shade."

PERCY BYSSHE SHELLEY

ONENESS

"Good-night? Ah! No; the hour is ill
Which severs those it should unite;
Let us remain together still,
Then it will be good night."

"See the mountains kiss the high heaven
And the waves clasp one another;
No sister-flower would be forgiven
If it disdained its brother;
And the sunlight clasps the earth,
And the moonbeams kiss the sea—
What is all this sweet work worth
If thou kiss not me?"

ANNA LETITIA BARBAULD

"We neither laugh alone, nor weep alone,
why then should we pray alone?"

SAMUEL TAYLOR COLERIDGE

"A great mind must be androgynous."

ALFRED DE MUSSET

"I don't know where my road is going,
but I know that I walk better when I
hold your hand."

VICTOR HUGO

PEACE

"Who among us has not sought peace
in a song?"

VICTOR HUGO

PERSEVERANCE

"Perseverance, secret of all triumphs."

ROBERT BROWNING

POSITIVITY

"Grow old along with me!
The best is yet to be,
The last of life,
For which the first was made.
Our times are in His hand who saith,
'A whole I planned, youth shows but half;
Trust God: see all, nor be afraid!'"

LORD BYRON

"They never fail who die in a great cause."

VICTOR HUGO

"Whatever causes night in our souls
may leave stars."

"Even the darkest night will end and
the sun will shine."

SAMUEL TAYLOR COLERIDGE PRAYER

"He prayeth best who lovest best."

VICTOR HUGO

"Prayer is an august avowal of ignorance."

"Those who always pray are necessary to those who never pray."

"Certain thoughts are prayer. There are moments when, whatever be the attitude of the body, the soul is on its knees."

LORD BYRON

"But words are things, and a small drop of ink,
Falling like dew, upon a thought, produces
That which makes thousands, perhaps millions, think."

CHARLOTTE TURNER SMITH

"It has been said that Shakespeare, the great delineator of human character, has failed in distinguishing his principal women—and that such as he meant to be amiable are all equally gentle and good. How difficult then it is for a novelist to give to one of his heroines any very marked feature which shall not disfigure her! Too much reason and self-command destroy the interest we take in her distresses. It has been observed that Clarissa is so equal to every trial as to diminish our pity. Other virtues than gentleness, pity, filial obedience, or faithful attachment, hardly belong to the sex."

SAMUEL TAYLOR COLERIDGE

"There is one art of which people should be masters—the art of reflection."

CHARLOTTE TURNER SMITH

"Ah! candid and unadulterated mind! you have learned early to reflect; but take care lest this habit, hitherto so well applied, should totally unfit you for society. It will strew thorns in your path, while other young women of your age seek only flowers. By imagining yourself in the place of others, as you now continually do, you will learn to feel for all the unhappy, or even for those who appear so; whereas it might save a great deal of (for the most part useless) pain, if you could contrive to feel only for yourself."

VICTOR HUGO

"Change your opinions, keep your principles; change your leaves, keep intact your roots."

WILLIAM WORDSWORTH

RESILIENCE

"Success consists of getting up just one more time than you fall."

WILLIAM BLAKE

RESPONSIBILITY

"The apple tree never asks the beech how he shall grow, nor the lion, the horse, how he shall take his prey."

"Enlightenment means taking full responsibility for your life."

VICTOR HUGO

"When dictatorship is a fact, revolution becomes a right."

VICTOR HUGO — RIGHTNESS

"Right is right only when entire."

PERCY BYSSHE SHELLEY — SELF-KNOWING

"People should riot for their freedom, but first they have to understand who they are and how they are ruled."

CHARLES LAMB — SIMPLICITY

"Cultivate simplicity, or rather I should say, banish elaborateness, for simplicity springs spontaneous from the heart."

VICTOR HUGO

SINCERITY

"As for methods of prayer, all of them are good as long as they are sincere."

LORD BYRON

"Sincerity may be humble but she cannot be servile."

WILLIAM WORDSWORTH

SOLITUDE

"When from our better selves we have too long
been parted by the hurrying world and droop,
sick of its business, or its pleasure tired,
how gracious, how benign is solitude."

VICTOR HUGO

SYMPATHY

"When the heart is dry the eye is dry."

"Never laugh at those who suffer;
suffer sometimes those who laugh."

JOHN KEATS

VENTURESOMENESS

"... I leaped headlong into the Sea, and thereby have become more acquainted with the Soundings, the quicksands, and the rocks, than if I had stayed upon the green shore, and piped a silly pipe, and took tea and comfortable advice."

ANNA LAETITIA BARBAULD

"Wisdom! I bless thy gentle sway, and ever, ever will obey."

WILLIAM BLAKE

"A fool sees not the same tree that a wise man sees."

WILLIAM WORDSWORTH

"Wisdom is oft-times nearer when we stoop than when we soar."

ROBERT BROWNING

"Success in marriage is more than finding the right person: it is being the right person."

SAMUEL TAYLOR COLERIDGE

"Common sense in an uncommon degree is what the world calls wisdom."

ROBERT BROWNING

"One wise man's verdict outweighs all the fools.'"

PERCY BYSSHE SHELLEY

"The wise want love; and those who love want wisdom."

WILLIAM WORDSWORTH

"Though nothing will bring back the hour of splendor in the grass, of glory in the flower, we will grieve not, rather find strength in what remains behind."

FELICIA DOROTHEA HEMANS

CASABIANCA (1826)

"The boy stood on the burning deck,
Whence all but he had fled;
The flame that lit the battle's wreck,
Shone round him o'er the dead.

Yet beautiful and bright he stood,
As born to rule the storm;
A creature of heroic blood,
A proud, though childlike form.

The flames roll'd on—he would not go,
Without his father's word;
That father, faint in death below,
His voice no longer heard.

He called aloud:—'Say, father, say
If yet my task is done?'
He knew not that the chieftain lay
Unconscious of his son.

'Speak, father!' once again he cried
'If I may yet be gone!'
And but the booming shots replied,
And fast the flames roll'd on.

Upon his brow he felt their breath,
And in his waving hair,
And looked from that lone post of death,
In still yet brave despair.

And shouted but once more aloud,
'My father, must I stay?'
While o'er him fast, through sail and shroud,
The wreathing fires made way.

They wrapt the ship in splendour wild,
They caught the flag on high,
And streamed above the gallant child,
Like banners in the sky.

There came a burst of thunder sound—
The boy—oh! where was he?
Ask of the winds that far around
With fragments strewed the sea!

With mast, and helm, and pennon fair,
That well had borne their part—
But the noblest thing which perished there,
Was that young faithful heart."

VERSE 3—

VICES

WILLIAM WORDSWORTH

"Society has parted man from man, neglectful of the universal heart."

CHARLOTTE TURNER SMITH

"I might, indeed, read history; but whenever I attempt to do so, I am... driven from it by disgust—What is it, but a miserably mortifying detail of crimes and follies?—of the guilt of a few, and the sufferings of many, while almost every page offers an argument in favor of what I never will believe—that heaven created the human race only to destroy itself."

ANNA LAETITIA BARBAULD

"It is, in truth, the most absurd of all suppositions, that a human being can be educated, or even nourished and brought up, without imbibing numberless prejudices from every thing which passes around him."

SAMUEL TAYLOR COLERIDGE

"This world has angels all too few, and heaven is overflowing."

VICTOR HUGO

"A criminal remains a criminal whether he uses a convict's suit or a monarch's crown."

"The wicked envy and hate; it is their way of admiring."

PERCY BYSSHE SHELLEY

"The person who has been accustomed to subdue men by force will be less inclined to the trouble of convincing or persuading them."

VICTOR HUGO
CARPING

"Be happy without picking flaws."

VICTOR HUGO
CONDEMNATION

"One sees qualities at a distance and defects at close range."

SAMUEL TAYLOR COLERIDGE
CONTEMPT

"Contempt is egotism in ill-humor."

ALPHONSE DE LAMARTINE CORRUPTION

"The more I see the representatives of the people, the more I admire my dogs."

SAMUEL TAYLOR COLERIDGE

"Oh, worse than everything, is kindness counterfeiting absent love."

WILLIAM BLAKE CUNNING

"The weak in courage is strong in cunning."

WILLIAM WORDSWORTH

DEFACING

"Pictures deface walls more often than they decorate them."

CHARLES LAMB

DEFAMATION

"Trample not on the ruins of a man."

VICTOR HUGO

DEGRADATION

"A fall from such a height is rarely straight downwards."

SAMUEL TAYLOR COLERIDGE

"As long as there are readers to be delighted with calumny, there will be found reviewers to calumniate."

VICTOR HUGO

"What a gloomy thing, not to know the address of one's soul."

WILLIAM BLAKE

"If the Sun and Moon should ever doubt, they'd immediately go out."

SAMUEL TAYLOR COLERIDGE

EGO

"Milton has carefully marked in his Satan the intense selfishness, the alcohol of egotism, which would rather reign in hell than serve in heaven."

JOHN KEATS

"It's better to lose your Ego to the One you Love than to lose the One you Love to your Ego."

SAMUEL TAYLOR COLERIDGE

EVIL

"The doing evil to avoid an evil cannot be good."

WILLIAN BLAKE

EXCESS

"The road of excess leads to the palace of wisdom.... You never know what is enough until you know what is more than enough."

VICTOR HUGO

FALSITY

"Between the government which does evil and the people who accept it there is a certain shameful solidarity."

"To live a life which is a perpetual falsehood is to suffer unknown tortures."

JOHN KEATS

GOSSIP

"To silence gossip, don't repeat it."

WILLIAM WORDSWORTH

GUILT

"From the body of one guilty deed a thousand ghostly fears and haunting thoughts proceed."

WILLIAM WORDSWORTH

HABIT

"Habit rules the unreflecting herd."

VICTOR HUGO

"Habit is the nursery of errors."

CHARLES LAMB

HATE

"Don't introduce me to that man! I
want to go on hating him, and I can't
hate a man whom I know."

LORD BYRON

HOLIER THAN THOU

"Of all the horrid, hideous notes of woe,
Sadder than owl-songs or the midnight blast;
Is that portentous phrase, 'I told you so.'"

VICTOR HUGO IDLENESS

"Idleness is a mother. She has a son, robbery, and a daughter, hunger."

"Idleness is the heaviest of oppressions."

VICTOR HUGO IGNORANCE

"The earth is a great piece of stupidity."

WILLIAM BLAKE ILL-INTENTION

"A truth that's told with bad intent,
Beats all the lies you can invent."

WILLIAM BLAKE

IMMOVABILITY

"Expect poison from the standing water."

"The man who never alters his opinion is the standing water, and breeds reptiles of the mind."

ALFRED DE MUSSET

"Few persons enjoy real liberty; we are all slaves to ideas or habits."

ROBERT BROWNING

INACTION

"But there are times when patience proves at fault."

VICTOR HUGO

"The spirit of God, like the sun, always gives all its light at once. The spirit of man resembles the pale moon, which has its phases, its absences and its returns, its lucidity and its spots, its fullness and its disappearance, which borrows all its light from the rays of the sun and which still dares to intercept them on occasion."

ALPHONSE DE LAMARTINE

"We cannot have two hearts, one for the animals and one for men. In cruelty towards the former and cruelty to the latter there is no difference but in the victim."

ROBERT BROWNING

INTOLERANCE

"There are those who believe in something, and therefore will tolerate nothing; and on the other hand, those who tolerate everything, because they believe in nothing."

SAMUEL TAYLOR COLERIDGE

"I have seen gross intolerance shown in support of tolerance."

VICTOR HUGO

LOQUACITY

"There are many tongues to talk, and but few heads to think."

VICTOR HUGO LYING

"To lie a little is not possible; he who lies, lies the whole lie."

VICTOR HUGO MEDDLING

"For prying into any human affairs, none are equal to those whom it does not concern."

SAMUEL TAYLOR COLERIDGE RAGE

"Rage is essentially vulgar."

SAMUEL TAYLOR COLERIDGE — REMORSE

"Remorse is as the heart in which it grows;
If it can be gentle, it drops balmy dews
Of true repentance;
But if proud and gloomy,
It is the poison tree, that pierced to the inmost,
Weeps only tears of poison."

SAMUEL TAYLOR COLERIDGE — SILENCE

"Silence does not always mark wisdom."

VICTOR HUGO

"It is not so easy to keep silent when
the silence is a lie."

PERCY BYSSHE SHELLEY

SLAVERY

"All spirits are enslaved which serve things evil."

VICTOR HUGO

SOURING

"In saying no to progress, it is not the future which they condemn, but themselves. They give themselves a melancholy disease; they inoculate themselves with the past. There is but one way of refusing tomorrow, that is to die."

SAMUEL TAYLOR COLERIDGE

"Indignation at literary wrongs I leave to men born under happier stars. I cannot afford it."

ELIZABETH BARRETT BROWNING

"We get no good
By being ungenerous, even to a book.

SAMUEL TAYLOR COLERIDGE

TORMENT

"Persecution is a very easy form of virtue."

LORD BYRON

VANITY

'Tis pleasant, sure, to see one's name
in print. A book's a book, although
there's nothing in it."

CHARLOTTE TURNER SMITH

"Ah! Thus man spoils Heaven's glorious works with blood."

VICTOR HUGO

"War, made by humanity, upon humanity, despite humanity."

ALPHONSE DE LAMARTINE

"Civil wars leave nothing but tombs."

VICTOR HUGO

"Civil war.... What did the words mean? Was there any such thing as a 'foreign war'? Was not all warfare between men warfare between brothers?"

SAMUEL TAYLOR COLERIDGE

"How like herrings and onions our vices are in the morning after we have committed them."

VICTOR HUGO

"When God desires to destroy a thing, he entrusts its destruction to the thing itself. Every bad institution of this world ends by suicide."

VERSE 4— THE BEAMS OF LOVE

ALFRED DE MUSSET

"I see that you believe in love such as the poets and romancers have represented.... The poets represent love as the sculptors design beauty, as the musicians create melody; that is to say, endowed with an exquisite nervous organization, they gather up with discerning ardor the purest elements of life, the most beautiful lines of matter, and the most harmonious voices of nature...."

WILLIAM BLAKE

"We are put on this earth a little space that we might learn to bear the beams of love."

VICTOR HUGO

"Life is the flower for which love is the honey."

PERCY BYSSHE SHELLEY

"Nothing in the word is single,
All things by law divine,
In one spirit meet and mingle—
Why not I with thine?"

VICTOR HUGO

"To love another person is to see the face of God."

ROBERT BROWNING

"I was made and meant to look for you and wait for you and become yours forever."

"If you are asking if I'd hurt you, the answer is never.
If you are asking if I love you, the answer is forever.
If you are asking if I want you, the answer is I do
If you are asking what I value most, the answer is YOU."

ELIZABETH BARRETT BROWNING

"The face of all the world is changed, I think
Since first I heard the footsteps of thy soul."

"I love you not only for what you are, but for what I am when I am with you."

FELICIA DOROTHEA HEMANS

"There is in all this cold and hollow world
No fount of deep, strong, deathless love
Save that within a mother's heart."

ALPHONSE DE LAMARTINE

"God has placed the genius of women in their hearts, because the works of his genius are always works of love."

"To love for the sake of being loved is human, but to love for the sake of loving is angelic."

SAMUEL TAYLOR COLERIDGE

"A woman's friendship borders more closely on love than man's. Men affect each other in the reflection of noble or friendly acts; whilst women ask fewer proofs and more signs and expressions of attachment."

VICTOR HUGO

"The supreme ordeal, let us say rather, the only ordeal, is the loss of the beloved being."

ALFRED DE MUSSET

"Take love as a sober man takes wine; do not become a drunkard. If your mistress is sincere and faithful, love her for that; but if she is not, if she is merely young and beautiful, love her for that; if she is agreeable and spiritual, love her for that; if she is none of these things but merely loves you, love her for that."

SAMUEL TAYLOR COLERIDGE

"Stimulate the heart to love and the mind to be early accurate, and all other virtues will rise of their own accord, and all vices will be thrown out."

VICTOR HUGO

"You can give without loving, but you can never love without giving. The great acts of love are done by those who are habitually performing small acts of kindness. We pardon to the extent that we love. Love is knowing that even when you are alone, you will never be lonely again. And great happiness of life is the conviction that we are loved. Loved for ourselves and even loved in spite of ourselves."

ANNA LAETITIA BARBAULD

"All those who love Nature she loves in return, and will richly reward, not perhaps with the good things, as they are commonly called, but with the best things, of this world; not with money and titles, horses and carriages, but with bright and happy thoughts, contentment and peace of mind."

WILLIAM WORDSWORTH

"There's a comfort in the strength of love;
'Twill make a thing endurable,
Which else would overset the brain, or
break the heart."

"Love betters what is best."

WILLIAM BLAKE

"He whose face gives no light, shall never become a star."

VICTOR HUGO

"If people did not love one another, I really don't see what use there would be in having any spring."

"If nobody loved, the sun would go out."

ROBERT BROWNING

"Take away love and our earth is a tomb."

VICTOR HUGO

"Woe, alas, to those who have loved only bodies, forms, appearances! Death will rob them of everything. Try to love souls, you will find them again."

"There are fathers who do not love their children; there is no grandfather who does not adore his grandson."

LORD BYRON

"There are four questions of value in life, Don Octavio. What is sacred? Of what is the spirit made? What is worth living for and what is worth dying for? The answer to each is the same. Only love."

VERSE 5 — THE GLOW OF BEAUTY

WILLIAM BLAKE

"Exuberance is beauty."

"Mere enthusiasm is the all-in-all....
Passion and expression are beauty itself."

JOHN KEATS

"A thing of beauty is a joy forever."

PERCY BYSSHE SHELLEY

"Know what it is to be a child? It is to be something very different from the man of today. It is to have a spirit yet streaming from the waters of Baptism; it is to believe in belief; it is to be so little that elves can reach to whisper in your ear; it is to turn pumpkins into coaches and mice into horses, lowness into loftiness, and nothing into everything, for each child had its fairy godmother in its soul."

VICTOR HUGO

"Ecclesiastes names thee Almighty, the Maccabees name thee Creator, the Epistle to the Ephesians names thee Liberty, Baruch names thee Immensity, the Psalms name thee Wisdom and Truth, John names thee Light, the Book of Kings names thee Lord, Exodus names thee Providence, Leviticus, Sanctity, Esdras, Justice, creation names thee God, man names thee Father; but Solomon names thee Compassion, which is the most beautiful of all thy names."

VICTOR HUGO

"A house is built of logs and stone, of
tiles and posts and piers; a home
is built of loving deeds that stand a
thousand years."

ROBERT BROWNING

"Open my heart and you will see
Graved inside of it, 'Italy.'"

PERCY BYSSHE SHELLEY

"Venice, its temples and palaces did
seem like fabrics of enchantment
piled to heaven."

VICTOR HUGO

"A breath of Paris preserves the soul."

PERCY BYSSHE SHELLEY

"Away, away, from men and towns,
To the wild wood and the downs,
To the silent wilderness,
Where the soul need not repress its music."

PERCY BYSSHE SHELLEY

"There is eloquence in the tongueless wind, and a melody in the flowing brooks and the rustling of the reeds beside them, which by their inconceivable relation to something within the soul, awaken the spirits to a dance of breathless rapture, and bring tears of mysterious tenderness to the eyes, like the enthusiasm of patriotic success, or the voice of one beloved singing to you alone."

FELICIA DOROTHEA HEMANS

"Ye may trace my step o'er the wakening earth,
By the winds which tell of the violet's birth,
By the primrose-stars in the shadowy grass,
By the green leaves, opening as I pass."

WILLIAM WORDSWORTH

"I wandered lonely as a cloud
That floats on high o'er vales and hills
When all at once I saw a crowd
A host of golden daffodils
Beside the lake beneath the trees
Fluttering and dancing in the breeze."

"Nature never did betray
The heart that loved her."

PERCY BYSSHE SHELLEY

"And the Spring arose on the garden fair,
Like the Spirit of Love felt everywhere;
And each flower and herb on Earth's dark breast
Rose from the dreams of its wintry rest."

WILLIAM WORDSWORTH

"For I have learned to look on nature, not as in the hour of thoughtless youth; but hearing oftentimes the still, sad music of humanity."

WILLIAM WORDSWORTH

"A lake carries you into recesses of feeling otherwise impenetrable."

JOHN KEATS

"I almost wish we were butterflies and liv'd but three summer days—three such days with you I could fill with more delight than fifty common years could ever contain."

VICTOR HUGO

"Everything speaks: the flowing airstream and the sailing halcyon, the blade of grass, the flower, the bud, the element; did you imagine the earth to be otherwise?"

LORD BYRON

"There is pleasure in the pathless woods, there is rapture in the lonely shore, there is society where none intrudes, by the deep sea, and music in its roar; I love Man the less, but Nature more."

JOHN KEATS

"Beauty is truth, truth beauty—that is all Ye know on earth, and all ye need to know."

"If something is not beautiful, it is probably not true."

"I never can feel certain of any truth, but from a clear perception of its beauty."

VICTOR HUGO

"To rise from error to truth is rare and beautiful."

LORD BYRON

"Truth is a gem that is found at great depth; whilst on the surface of the world all things are weighed by the false scale of custom."

VICTOR HUGO

"The beautiful is as useful as the useful... perhaps more so."

VERSE 6—

CODA

VICTOR HUGO

"I advance in life, I grow more simple, and I become more patriotic for humanity."

WILLIAM WORDSWORTH

"What we have loved, others will love, and we will teach them how; instruct them how the mind of man becomes a thousand times more beautiful than the earth on which he dwells."

PERCY BYSSHE SHELLEY

"I love Love—though he has wings,
And like light can flee,
But above all other things,
Spirit, I love thee—
Thou art love and life! O come!
Make once more my heart thy home."

PERCY BYSSHE SHELLEY

"For love and beauty and delight, there is no death nor change."

LORD BYRON

"Be thou the rainbow in the storms of life. The evening beam that smiles the clouds away, and tints tomorrow with prophetic ray."

WILLIAM BLAKE

"Celebrate your existence!"

VICTOR HUGO

"A cannonball travels only two thousand miles an hour; light travels two hundred thousand miles a second. Such is the superiority of Jesus Christ over Napoleon."

WILLIAM BLAKE

"Everything that lives, lives not alone, nor for itself."

JOHN KEATS

"Don't be discouraged by a failure. It can be a positive experience. Failure, is, in a sense, the highway to success, inasmuch as every discovery of what is false leads us to seek earnestly after what is true, and every fresh experience points out some form of error which we shall afterwards carefully avoid."

ROBERT BROWNING

"Measure your mind's height by the shade it casts."

PERCY BYSSHE SHELLEY

"To suffer woes which Hope thinks infinite;
To forgive wrongs darker than Death or Night;
To defy Power, which seems Omnipotent;
To love, and bear; to hope till Hope creates
From its own wreck the thing it contemplates;
Neither to change, nor falter, nor repent;
This, like thy glory, Titan, is to be
Good, great and joyous, beautiful and free;
This is alone Life, Joy, Empire, and Victory!"

VICTOR HUGO

"Winter is on my head, but eternal spring is in my heart. The nearer I approach the end, the plainer I hear around me the immortal symphonies of the worlds which invite me.... For half a century I have been writing thoughts in prose, verse, history, drama, romance, tradition, satire, ode, and song. I have tried them all, but I feel I have not said a thousandth part of that which is within me. When I go down to the grave, I can say 'I have finished my day's work,' but I cannot say 'I have finished my life's work.'"

"My day's work will begin again the next morning."

ANNA LAETITIA BARBAULD

"Life! we've been long together,
Through pleasant and through cloudy weather;
'Tis hard to part when friends are dear;
Perhaps 'twill cost a sigh, a tear;
Then steal away, give little warning.
Choose thine own time;
Say not 'Good-night,' but in some brighter clime
Bid me 'Good-morning.'"

ALFRED DE MUSSET

"With a kiss, let us set out for an
unknown world."

FELICIA DOROTHEA HEMANS

"THE BETTER LAND"

"I hear thee speak of the better land,
Thou call'st its children a happy band;
Mother! oh, where is that radiant shore?—
Shall we not seek it, and weep no more?—
Is it where the flower of the orange blows,
And the fire-flies glance through the myrtle-boughs?"
—"Not there, not there, my child!"

"Is it where the feathery palm-trees rise,
And the date grows ripe under sunny skies?—
Or 'midst the green islands of glittering seas,
Where fragrant forests perfume the breeze,
And strange, bright birds, on their starry wings,
Bear the rich hues of all glorious things?"
—"Not there, not there, my child!"

"Is it far away, in some region old,
Where the rivers wander o'er sands of gold?—
Where the burning rays of the ruby shine,
And the diamond lights up the secret mine,
And the pearl gleams forth from the coral strand—
Is it there, sweet mother, that better land?"
—"Not there, not there, my child!"

"Eye hath not seen it, my gentle boy!
Ear hath not heard its deep songs of joy;
Dreams cannot picture a world so fair—
Sorrow and death may not enter there;
Time doth not breathe on its fadeless bloom,
For beyond the clouds, and beyond the tomb,
—It is there, it is there, my child!"

SPEAKER

BIOGRAPHIES

SPEAKER BIRTHPLACE

DURHAM

COCKERMOUTH

LIVERPOOL

LEICESTERSHIRE

LONDON

HORSHAM

OTTERY ST. MARY

PARIS

BESANÇON

MÂCON

DURHAM
ELIZABETH BARRETT BROWNING 1806-1861

COCKERMOUTH
WILLIAM WORDSWORTH 1770-1850

LIVERPOOL
FELICIA DOROTHEA BROWNE HEMANS 1793-1835

LEICESTERSHIRE
ANNA LAETITIA BARBAULD 1743-1825

LONDON
CHARLOTTE TURNER SMITH 1749-1806
WILLIAM BLAKE 1757-1827
CHARLES LAMB 1775-1834
LORD BYRON 1788-1824
JOHN KEATS 1795-1821
ROBERT BROWNING 1812-1889

HORSHAM
PERCY BYSSHE SHELLEY 1792-1822

OTTERY ST. MARY
SAMUEL TAYLOR COLERIDGE 1771-1834

PARIS
ALFRED DE MUSSET 1810-1857

BESANÇON
VICTOR HUGO 1802-1885

MÂCON
ALPHONSE DE LAMARTINE 1790-1869

1743-1825

ANNA LAETITIA BARBAULD

Was born Anna Laetitia Aikin at Kibworth Harcourt, Leicestershire, England. She was a prominent poet, writer, critic, editor and educator. In 1773, her first book, *Poems,* gave an instant reputation. She and her husband, Rochemont Barbauld, felt they would be childless so she suggested to her brother that they adopt one of his children. For whatever reason, the brother agreed. Her lasting books, *Lessons for Children* (1778-79) and *Hymns in Prose for Children* (1781), were written for new son Charles. The latter book went through thirty editions by 1849. Meanwhile, Rochemont became increasingly unstable mentally with bouts of fury against Anna. Once with a knife, he chased her round the dinner table, and she escaped by leaping out a window. She stayed with him till he drowned himself. Anna opposed slavery and promoted humanity, peace, liberty and affectionate devotion. She was one of the founders of Romanticism, but her book *Eighteen Hundred and Eleven* in 1812 turned other Romantic poets against her because it criticized Britain as a waning imperial power. She was demeaned as "only" a children's writer in the 19th century, and mostly forgotten in the 20th until feminist literary criticism of the 1980s restored her rightful place in English literature.

1757-1827

WILLIAM BLAKE

Born in Soho, London, was the most strikingly original and earliest of the male Romantic poets, though largely unrecognized in life. A remarkable artist and engraver, he was also clairvoyant. "I am under the direction of Messengers from Heaven Daily & Nightly," Blake said. He was influenced by Emanuel Swedenborg, the Swedish mystic. He abhorred institutionalized religion; his religion was a private communion with Spirit. His works inspired musical composers, including Hubert Parry who made Blake's poem, "Jerusalem," the beautiful and unofficial anthem of England. The day he died, seeing his wife Catherine in tears, he cried, "Stay Kate! Keep just as you are—I will draw your portrait—for you have ever been an angel to me." He promised to be with her always, then sang hymns and verses till near the end.

ELIZABETH BARRETT BROWNING

Born in Durham, England, wrote poetry when she was 6 or 7. A spinal injury at age 15 made her a virtual invalid. Her first book, *An Essay on Mind, and Other Poems* arrived in 1826, and by the time her book *Poems* came in 1844, she was a national figure. "To Elizabeth Barrett Browning," a scholar wrote, "belongs the double honor of being one of the two or three most distinguished woman poets in English literature and the heroine of the most celebrated romance in English literary history." Robert Browning admired her. His first letter to her in January 1845 said: "Love your verses with all my heart, dear Miss Barrett." He added, "I love you too." The love proved mutual. Elizabeth's doctor advised Italy for her health but her stern father disallowed it, and he forbade her marriage. Secretly, the couple married in September 1846, and left for Italy. There she wrote two books sealing her affection for Italy. They had a son and fifteen happy years together. Her ever-fragile health broke again, and she died in Robert's arms on 29 June, 1861, Browning said, "smilingly, happily, with a face like a girl's." Her final word—"Beautiful."

1812-1889

ROBERT BROWNING

Born in London, was a second generation Romantic. He had little formal education, but *Italy* was his education, and his father's library was too. He fell in love with poet Elizabeth Barrett, and in 1846 they married and left for Italy, eventually Florence. A pundit called Browning, "one of the great affirmative voices of English." His cherished "Love Among the Ruins" contemplates a vanished empire where "one year they sent a million fighters forth… with their triumphs and their glories and the rest." On the same field, Browning sees "a girl with eager eyes and yellow hair…[who] waits for me…." Which is finest—the glory of an empire that time destroyed, or love that lives forever? "Love is best," he decides. Browning is buried in Poet's Corner, Westminster Abbey, beside Alfred Lord Tennyson.

1788-1824

LORD BYRON

Born in London, England, was one of the greatest English poets. A commentator called him "the finest satirical poet since Pope." His *Childe Herold's Pilgrimage* appeared in 1812 to instant acclaim. "I awoke one morning," he said, "and found myself famous." His masterwork, Percy Shelley said, was *Don Juan*, adventures in sixteen thousand captivating lines. Socially, he exhibited unbridled sexuality and endless affairs including with his half sister. He married Annabella Milbank in 1815, they had a daughter in December, and she left him in January. Bruised and discredited, he abandoned England forever in April 1816. He spent seven years in Italy. He also learned Armenian, co-authored a grammar in English and Armenian, and translated the *Epistle of Paul to the Corinthians* in Armenian.Then he sold his Rochdale Manor estate in England to fund Greek independence. He commanded a rebel army, but fell ill with fever and died on 19 April, 1824. Even now, the Greeks revere him as no other foreigner. His remains were taken to Westminster Abbey, but refused on moral grounds. As he lay in state, huge crowds viewed his coffin. He is buried at the Church of St. Mary Magdalene, Nottinghamshire. In 1969 a memorial was granted him in Westminster Abbey.

1771-1834

SAMUEL TAYLOR COLERIDGE

Born in Ottery St. Mary, Devonshire, England, and partnered with William Wordsworth, ushered in the Romantic era with *Lyrical Ballads*. The most diversified of the British Romantics, he was a philosopher, critic, theologian and poet. He even joined the poet Robert Southey in a venture, later dropped, to create a utopian society in the wilds of Pennsylvania. Unhappily, his health was poor, and he became addicted to opium and stretches of depression. This instability is felt in his "Dejection—An Ode." Yet, Coleridge was very interested in the conflict between good and evil and the appreciation of the beauty of all living things, themes in his best-known work, "The Rime of the Ancient Mariner." "He prayeth best who loveth best, All things both great and small," he wrote. Overall, "his was the most fertile and stimulating mind of his generation," an observer said.

1793-1835

FELICIA DOROTHEA BROWNE HEMANS

Born in Liverpool, England, wrote twenty-four volumes of poetry from 1816 to 1834. Even when young, she could repeat pages of poetry word for word that she had just read. At age 19 she married Capt. Alfred Hemans, and bore five sons before separating, somehow amicably, when all the boys were under 6 years old. Her writings sustained the broken family. "Casabianca," likely her best known poem, appears in this book. Her memorials to King George III and to Princess Charlotte treated the madness of the king kindly and sensitively. She was a writer for common folk, women particularly. In "The Better Land," also reproduced in this book, a mother, in despair at rampant illness and high infant and maternal death rates, wonders where is that "radiant shore" where weeping and death end. Greatly distressed by her mother's death in 1827, she became an invalid, suffering from an enclosed life and a weak heart. She died in Dublin at age 41.

1802-1885

VICTOR HUGO

Born in Besançon, France, was immensely prolific as a poet, dramatist, and novelist. He was the most important of the French Romantics. He married his childhood friend, Adèle Foucher, and they had five children. He disliked the church for its straightjacketing of faith, but he was very spiritual. In the decade after 1830, he published four books of poetry and *The Hunchback of Notre Dame*. In 1862 he published *Les Misérables*. From academics to commoners, he had a way of touching all hearts. He spoke for the poor, for women, and for the ending of capital punishment. Opposed to autocrat, Napoleon III, he fled to the British isles of Jersey and Guernsey in exile from 1851 to 1870. The day after the Republic was reborn, he returned to France, a national hero. When he died, he was given a state funeral. On the procession to the Pantheon, his burial place, two thousand delegates, and two million more, sadly saluted the greatest French writer of the century.

1795-1821

JOHN KEATS

Born in London, went to school at Enfield. There the master, Reverend John Clarke, noted, "His passions at times were almost ungovernable, [but] not merely was he 'the favorite of all,' like a pet prize-fighter, for his terrier courage; but his high-mindedness, his utter unconsciousness of a mean motive, his placability, his generosity, wrought so general a feeling... that I never heard a word of disapproval from anyone...." Keats earned a licence to practice medicine, but after 1817, he focused entirely on poetry. The brutal criticisms of his early work he met with self-confident steadiness. He fell in love with Fanny Brawne in 1818, and despite his initial carping, he saw her innate beauty, and they were secretly engaged. The first nine months of 1819 he composed his finest work, his great odes and verse romances. Then his tuberculosis grew apace. Seeking health in the warmth of Italy, he and a faithful friend went to Rome where he died in early 1821, aged 25 years. Fanny and he were to marry on his return to England. Less appreciated in his short life, his reputation grew in the coming decades.

1790-1869

ALPHONSE DE LAMARTINE

Was born in Mâcon, Burgundy, France, into French nobility. Some call him the first French Romantic poet. He was a pantheist, seeing God in everyone and everything. Many verses in his poetry are dedicated to the loves of his life. He helped found the Second Republic where he was basically head of the provisional government, and he facilitated the abolition of slavery and the death penalty. His *Histoire des Girondins* in 1847 was a major success. Some of his books in the 1850s, a scholar said, "remained unequalled," including his histories of Russia, Turkey, and the Restoration. By age 60, he was broken in health and finances, partly because of his generosity to his sisters in the property inheritance he received from his father's estate. To keep solvent, he published book after book, but he died poor and almost forgotten in Paris.

1775-1834

CHARLES LAMB

Born in London, was a fine poet, but an even finer essayist. His *Essays of Elia* spoke of a friendly, good-natured soul, like himself, nostalgic, fine-humored, compassionate. In 1808 he published *The Adventures of Ulysses*, a children's book. His famous poem, "The Old Familiar Faces," speaks of the loss of friends and loved ones, including his mother. "Where have they gone, the old familiar faces?" he asks, as every generation has asked. In 1796, his sister Mary, in a fit of insanity, murdered their mother, and Lamb cared for Mary the rest of his life. He befriended several Romantics, especially Coleridge and Wordsworth, and his biographer E.V. Lucas called him "the most lovable figure in English literature." In 1792 he fell in love with a young woman, wooed her for years, wrote many pieces about her, but she married another—his "great disappointment." Later, he fell in love with an actress, but she too refused him, and he died a bachelor and was buried in Edmonton, Middlesex, England.

1810-1857

ALFRED DE MUSSET

Born in Paris, was influenced in adolescence by French Romantic writers, including Victor Hugo. A great poet, he was more famous as a dramatist. His first work was *Stories of Spain and of Italy*, in 1830. He lived a life of feverish sexuality and alcoholic dissolution, often in brothels. His famous love affair with Georges Sand was celebrated in his *The Confession of a Child of the Century* (1836) and made into two films (1999 and 2012). His finest poems showed great dexterity and versatility and were often inspired by his love affairs. His *Lorenzaccio* was a dramatic masterpiece of the entire Romantic period. Set in 16th Century Florence, it follows a hero, once pure, but now less, ravaged by doubt and estranged from a world he sought to help. Musset was a brilliant satirist of current fashions, including Romantic excesses. In 1845, he accepted the highest award of merit in France—the *Legion d'honneur*. In 1852 he was elected to the French Academy that regulates the French language. Suffering from tuberculosis, he died in his sleep in Paris at age 46.

1792-1822

PERCY BYSSHE SHELLEY

Born in Field Place, near Horsham, Sussex, England, was called by the *College Survey of English Literature* "the greatest English poet of human perfectibility, the poet of ideal love and beauty informing all things, binding all things together...." His search for social justice and personal love produced poems of the first rank. In 1811 he eloped with Harriet Westbrook who in 1813 gave birth to their daughter. A year later, he eloped with Mary Godwin, and Harriet drowned herself. He was an atheist, but a humanist. His masterwork was *Prometheus Unbound*, about hope for a finer tomorrow, and his memorable poems included "Ode to the West Wind," "To a Skylark," and "Ozymandias," a symbol of the transiency of worldly power. Amid family upset, ill health, and anger at his atheism and his dismissal of social strictions, he left for Italy in 1818 where he wrote some of the most beautiful poems of the entire Romantic period. He died at sea in a fierce storm off Tuscany, at age 29.

1749-1806

CHARLOTTE TURNER SMITH

Born in London, was called the first Romantic poet. Her father gave her in marriage at age 15 to Benjamin Smith, a violent ne'er-do-well. Their relationship she condemned as legal prostitution, and she bore twelve children. The wealthy grandfather willed most of his property to Charlotte's children, but the will was challenged for forty years. Benjamin illegally spent a third of the legacy and ended in debtor's prison. Smith joined him and wrote *Elegiac Sonnets* in 1784 which funded their prison release. Ever fearful, Charlotte left him in 1787. But she didn't secure legal agreement to protect her book profits. So, to cover the will lawsuit and care for her children, she wrote novels. In ten years, she did ten. She noted the exploitation of women and called for equity. Her mother had died in childbirth when she was three, her first child died a day after her second was born, and six of her children died before her. So poor by 1803, she had to sell her beloved library. Famous for children's books, she was forgotten for a century before her novels reappeared in the feminist study. Near the end, she suffered terribly and had the "locomotive powers," she said, of a "cauliflower." When Benjamin died in February 1806, she got some of what he owed, but was too ill to benefit and died eight months later.

1770-1850

WILLIAM WORDSWORTH

Was born in Cockermouth, Cumberland, England. He lost his mother when he was 8, and his father five years later. In the summer recess of his schooling at Cambridge, he was overcome by a potent, near mystical dedication to poetry, the morning after a country dance. Three years on, he toured revolutionary France and was thrilled by the impulse of liberty, then appalled by the violence that ensued. His great decade, 1797-1808, began with his friendship with Samuel Taylor Coleridge. Together they introduced the Romantic advent in English poetry. He had a period of despair, then his beloved sister Dorothy, also an author and poet, lifted his spirits. Wordsworth focused on the link between the inner spirit of humanity and the outward world of nature. Happiness arose when a thoughtful mind was "wedded to this goodly universe in love and holy passion." Great human dignity and worth were part of that passion. In nature there was great beauty and truth, and thus great upliftment. "Our destiny, our being's heart and home," he said, "Is with infinitude, and only there." He was named Poet Laureate in 1843 and held the honor till his death.